Hands

Published by Olive Tree Book Company, an imprint of Greenleaf Book Group
4425 S. Mo Pac Expy., Suite 600
Austin, TX 78735

Distributed by Greenleaf Book Group LLC

For ordering information or special discounts for bulk purchases, please contact Greenleaf Book Group at 4425 S. Mo Pac Expy., Suite 600, Austin, TX 78735, (512) 891-6100.

Design and composition by Greenleaf Book Group LLC
Cover design by Greenleaf Book Group LLC

Publisher's Cataloging-In-Publication Data
(Prepared by The Donohue Group, Inc.)

Clements, Melinda.
  Hands / Melinda Clements.
    p. : ill. ; cm.
  ISBN: 978-1-929774-53-1
1. Hand--Religious aspects--Christianity--Fiction. 2. Hand--Pictorial works.
3. Christian fiction. I. Title.
PS3603.L465 H36 2008
813/.6   2007943209

Printed in China on acid-free paper

13 12 11 10 09 08   10 9 8 7 6 5 4 3 2 1

First Edition

Hands

Melinda Clements

Olive Tree
Book Company

AN IMPRINT OF
GREENLEAF BOOK GROUP LLC

An old man, probably some ninety-plus
years, sat hunched on a park bench. He
didn't move, just sat with his head down,
staring at his hands.

I sat down beside him, but he didn't acknowledge my presence. Finally, not really wanting to disturb him, but also wanting to check on him, I asked him if he was okay.

He raised his head and looked at me and smiled. "Yes, I'm fine. Thank you for asking," he said in a clear, strong voice.

"I didn't mean to disturb you, sir, but you were just sitting here staring at your hands, and I wanted to make sure you were alright," I explained to him.

"Have you ever looked at your hands?" he asked. "I mean really looked at your hands."

I slowly opened my hands and stared down at them. I turned them over, palms up and then palms down. *No, I guess I have never really looked at my hands*, I thought, as I tried to figure out the point he was making.

Then he smiled and began talking.

"Stop and think for a moment about the hands you have, how they have served you well throughout your years. These hands, though now wrinkled, shriveled, and weak, are the tools I have always used to reach out and grab and embrace life."

"They braced and caught my fall when as a toddler I crashed upon the floor. They tied my shoes and pulled on my boots. They put food in my mouth and clothes on my back. As a child I learned to fold them in prayer."

"They have covered my face, combed my hair, and cleansed my body. They have been sticky and wet, raw and dry. They sowed fields, brought in harvests, and lifted a plow off my best friend's foot."

"They wiped my tears and held my rifle when I went off to war. They wrote the letters home. They have been scraped and swollen, bent and broken. But they were strong and sure when I dug my buddy out of a foxhole."

ARMY
U-6 A
SERIAL NO.

"Decorated with my wedding band,
they showed the world that I was
married and loved someone special.
They caressed the love of my life, and
they were uneasy and clumsy when I
tried to hold my newborn daughter."

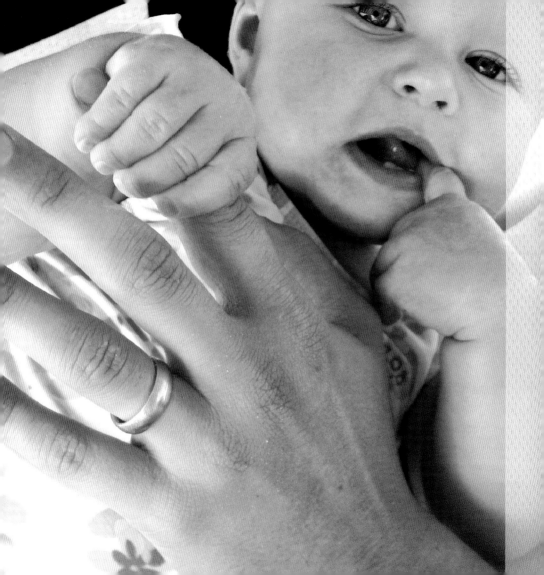

"They trembled and shook when I walked my daughter down the aisle. They grasped for each other at the funerals of my parents and spouse."

"They have tickled my sons, consoled neighbors, and shook in fists of anger."

"And to this day, when not much of anything else of me works real well, these hands hold me up, lay me down, and continue to fold in prayer."

"These hands are the mark of where I've been and the ruggedness of my life. But more importantly it will be these hands that God will reach out and take when He leads me home. And He won't care about where these hands have been or how they've helped me through life."

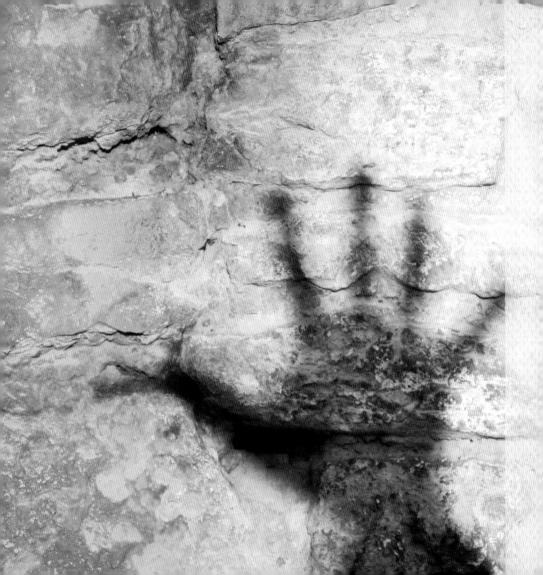

"What He will care about is how much he loves these hands and to whom they belong. He will lift me to His side and there I will use these hands to touch the face of Christ."

I never saw the old man again after I left the park that day, but I will never forget him and the words he spoke. No doubt I will never look at my hands the same again.

When my hands are hurt or sore or when I stroke the face of one of my children or my wife, I think of the man in the park. I have a feeling he has been stroked and caressed and held by the hands of God. I, too, want to touch the face of God and feel his hands upon my face. Thank you, Father, for hands.

Melinda Clements has been a teacher for seventeen
years. She is also a guitarist and freelance writer.
Incorporating her writing, her music, and her gift of
counseling, Melinda sends out daily devotionals online
and in a monthly newsletter. She is a member of the
American Association of Christian Counselors and lives
on a cattle ranch in West Texas.